T0128786

THIS IS INDIA

THIS IS INDIA

KAYE FISHER

authorHOUSE®

AuthorHouse™
1663 Liberty Drive
Bloomington, IN 47403
www.authorhouse.com
Phone: 1-800-839-8640

© 2012 by Kaye Fisher. All rights reserved.

No part of this book may be reproduced, stored in a retrieval system, or transmitted by any means without the written permission of the author.

Published by AuthorHouse   10/09/2012

ISBN: 978-1-4772-4138-7 (sc)
ISBN: 978-1-4772-4137-0 (e)

Library of Congress Control Number: 2012912710

Any people depicted in stock imagery provided by Thinkstock are models, and such images are being used for illustrative purposes only.
Certain stock imagery © Thinkstock.

This book is printed on acid-free paper.

Because of the dynamic nature of the Internet, any web addresses or links contained in this book may have changed since publication and may no longer be valid. The views expressed in this work are solely those of the author and do not necessarily reflect the views of the publisher, and the publisher hereby disclaims any responsibility for them.

CONTENTS

This book is dedicated to Adil and Kashmin

PREFACE

When I was travelling in the Scandinavian countries in 1983 I happened to meet a young East Indian, Adil (the same age as my son). This was before email, but we kept in touch by snail mail.

When I took early retirement from teaching in 1988, Adil wrote me to state, "You have been in so many parts of the world, why do you not come to India?" A seed was planted.

Adil was in Bombay at that time and after I had seen some of the other Asian countries I arrived in Bombay where Adil met me and had a hotel arranged for me.

We have continued our friendship ever since, much easier now with email.

THIS IS INDIA-1989

Although I spent a total of eight weeks (five weeks February-March, three weeks April-May) in India I know full well that I only touched the tip of the ice berg. And what I did experience is basically from visiting areas which many tourists visit. If my observations differ from others it may be because I am who I am.

From the mustachioed men to the sari-clad women; from the well-dressed business men flying Indian Airlines, that far from efficient form of transportation with umpteen different methods or lack thereof of airport security, to the numberless beggars who call a city sidewalk their abode; from the three air terminalled New Delhi to the lowly human drawn rickshaws of Amritsar or Calcutta; from the once-grandeur-of-English-rule hotels charging exorbitant rates (Great Eastern, Calcutta) to newly developed hotels charging comparatively little for fine rooms (Ronil Beach Resort, Goa and Casino Hotel, Cochin); from the over-zealous taxi or rickshaw driver who once he has a tourist aboard

1

increases the fare dramatically, especially if the fare has not been bargained upon first, to the most friendly, most helpful gentleman on the street who will walk blocks in order to see that you are aboard the city tour bus for the day; from the shoe shiner in the streets of Bombay with ten children to the houseboat owner in Srinagar whose one-year old daughter, truly doted upon, is the only child he wants; from the 37 degrees Celsius temperature experienced in Calcutta and Amritsar to the hailstorm and thunderstorm in Darjeeling, the like of which I have never witnessed before; from the society where graft is evidently rampant (no personal evidence) or payoffs or commission is received to take a sightseeing tourist to a shop, to the young teenage boys who unselfishly buy "chai" (tea) or sweets so that they may be sampled for the first time; from the extremely intelligent Indians (both men and women) who will undoubtedly ensure India of a finer future to the sari-dressed women involved in road construction, a primitive situation in a non-technological country. Yes, India is a land of contrasts: a land of extremes.

India is people everywhere! The caste system is most evident in traffic on a city street. Size dictates the right-of-way in transportation: buses and trucks fight it out for top priority, cars and taxis impose themselves above motorcycles, motorbikes, rickshaws, (motorized, bicycle, or human drawn,) bicycles, and animal or human drawn carts. And among all this congestion, for that is what develops as the sacred cow and pedestrians mingle in the slow-moving, horn-honking scene, one accepts his lot unperturbedly; indeed, with a measure of politeness: only occasional short-tempered outbursts are noted.

Country driving involves probably never driving much above 60 km an hour. Roads are narrow and must be shared with all means of transport: depending upon the region, bullock, oxen, cow, or camel drawn carts and the numerous cyclists and pedestrians.

Yes, people everywhere: from early morning ball players, joggers and exercisers along the marine drives, side-stepping the sleeping poverty-stricken, to the families who, in the cooling of evening engage in an after-late-dinner stroll. (Chowpatty Beach, Bombay, is particularly popular.) Or the energetic Sunday picknickers on Elephanta Island engaged in singing, dancing, games and delighting in having their photos taken. The Indians are truly family oriented: they appear to love their children dearly and the older grandparents are part of the nuclear family.

Although one tries not to see them and to maybe avoid them, actually a task utterly impossible, the maimed, the destitute, old and young, are everywhere: the young man with no legs who pushes himself with his arms about on a skateboard, the old mother leading a blind son, the young mother, looking old beyond her years, carrying a nigh-limp child, dirty waifs who pathetically reach out with one hand while motioning to their mouths with the other, older children carrying around younger ones, often pinching them to make them cry, or the brazen youngsters who ask for money, hoping this tourist is good for a rupee or two. Only once, and that on Juhu Beach, Bombay, did I find myself truly harassed by a begging woman who refused to take no for an answer. She persisted on plucking at my arm until I was forced to retreat to the restaurant area. Fortunately, the Indians themselves are generous with alms.

The generosity and hospitality of Indians endeared the race to me. I could cite example after example: a male seat companion on the bus en route from Bangalore to Mysore peeled a mandarin and then offered me half; a young couple on a bus tour shared their banana chips; an older couple from Calcutta insisted on paying for my lunch because I was a guest in their country; (Maybe they figured they owed it to me after seven adults and one child were squeezed along with the driver into the taxi tour for hours. At least this vehicle appeared roadworthy in contrast to the minibus of the day before when the gearshift stick continually separated from the gear box and in order to shut off the motor the driver pulled on a string! (Only in India!) Add to this the two young men working towards their M.A. in English who bought me "grounders" (peanuts) as we walked around Brindavan Gardens and then rushed with me to make certain I found my bus after the musical fountain display; the young men in Hassan who bought me the milky-sweet coffee (boiled together) before taking me to view the small Jain temple nearby and then concluded my "tour" by taking me to a milk-sweets shop where I

gratuitously sampled an Indian sweet for the first time;
Keith, the young Christian hotel employee in Madras
who showed genuine concern when I was ill, but when
he was off duty and I was feeling better walked along
the beach with me; the favour bestowed by the hotel
owner in Darjeeling when he took me along with his
wife and family to the Buddhist Monastery special
dance in nearby Ghoom and the resulting sincere
welcome by these monks; the nineteen year old girl in
Kalimpong who invited four of us out of the rain and
while we talked, her mother, who did not speak English,
prepared fried eggs, cookies and tea for us; the ten year
old shikara rower who quoted his fare "whatever you
like"—I bet he made money!—; the number of school
groups who usually eyed me curiously at first and then
gathered up their courage to speak with me and to ask
me to be in their group photo—and how delightful it
was when after our chat the boys all wanted to shake
hands with me. My family doctor at the time, Dr
Guhu's two sisters in Calcutta took great pains to meet
me; Adil, who met my plane and reserved a hotel room
when I first arrived in Bombay, and who escorted
me to truly Indian events, a one year old child's large
birthday party and to Anaheeta's Parsi wedding—both
opportunities to enjoy Indian food from banana leaf
"plates" (I did not have to eat with my fingers however.)
Then Adil's uncle delighted me with his scrapbook of
cycling around the world in the 1930's and his cousin's
wife who explained a number of Indian practices; and
Rusi and Sheroo, Adil's friends, in whose home I was
welcomed for several meals and ensured I visited many
parts of Bombay, including the Wall of Silence and Juhu
Beach.

To an outsider, at first glance, this decidedly overpopulated, decidedly non-technological country (antiquated telephone system, construction relies upon human brawn rather than the human brain, simple tasks, whether carrying crates of soft drinks or calculations in a bank, are accomplished the long, hard way) is one where to escape the vigours (and that is a nondescript term indeed!) would be the ambition of everyone.

But pride: this evident emotion is displayed in various guises: the twenty year old Abraham from a family of ten (and incidentally with a beautiful singing voice) who took me after our camel ride in Jaisalmer to his dirt-floored home to meet his grandparents and his uncle, an English teacher; Amin, the Srinagar houseboat owner and the deep pride he had in his heritage; Yusef, the twenty-three old drug-user-artist, fiercely proud of the artistic talents of his ten year old brother and who yearned to return to his hillside village outside Udaipur. A further example—the group of the young men typifying the "joie-de-vivre" of their country, so proud of the fact they were Indian, as they enjoyed an evening cultural performance as guests of the Japanese. Whereas India has lost intelligent people to other nations, there are still many who after a stint away have chosen to return to their motherland with very deep-seated pride.

It took awhile to accept the forthrightness of Indians: such outright questions as "How old are you?", "How much did you pay for this? are not asked of strangers in the West. But it seems to be part of most Indians' inquisitive nature, just as it is to move in to listen to others conversations, whether they could understand it or not. But soon I felt their personal questions were an indication of a genuine interest in me: in my status as a widow, a lone traveler. The much repeated "No problem", is a true indication of so many Indians' feelings—what the asker desires is as much as done when requested if it is at all within their capabilities. I grew to love the polite command, "Come", in contrast to our western term, "Let's go".

With only one exception, I felt completely safe in India. This was in the Red Fort in Old Delhi when I took a tour with a dozen or so people. I felt rather uneasy when a half dozen men continually circled around our group. As mentioned I travelled to Darjeeling, Kalimpong, Srinagar, and Amritsar where after reading about the unrest in some of these areas, I was thankful I had not encountered it firsthand.

Although I was able to accept and positively revel in several aspects of Indian culture, I found it very difficult to acknowledge the subservience of women. I did not openly complain, but I seethed when men pushed their air tickets or their telephone call sheets into the wicket ahead of everyone instead of queuing. Granted, such conceding politeness to women in the western world is disappearing, but in India, I would say it has never been practiced. Women are subordinate citizens and the majority accept this lot, but in my opinion, this is such a shame: their lithe sari-clad bodies (in the southern part at least, the northern women do tend to display that "spare tire".), their dark beauty requiring little or no make-up, their hair, black, usually beautifully long, often entwined with roses or frangipani, demand attention. Conversely, I question the beauty of jewellery inserted into noses or lips or even rings on toes, (An indication of some significance?) I must not forget to mention the veiled, (partially or completely) women noted particularly in the northwest.

The arranging of saris remains a mystery to me—I would dearly have liked to have modeled one. But an even greater enigma is how both men and women tie the "ballooning-legs" (dhotis) costume. I did not notice that many pregnant women, compared to Japan, for example. Was it because the sari is a fine disguise, don't pregnant women generally appear in public, or has birth control really become a reality?

But these men who assert top status—how beguiling are the black mustaches on their dark faces! I was told their mustache reveals their personality. Maybe so! Only in Calcutta were there a number of men without them. Another observation from which I can only draw my own unstated conclusions is that Indian males have a decided habit of openly grasping their trousers to rearrange their testicles.

I must not overlook citing a couple examples of the sense of humor I encountered. The airline employee who, on a hot, cloudless morning laughingly repeated "weather conditions" as the stated reason for the aircraft's delay; the desk clerk at the Y in Bombay, who, when I turned the wrong direction to walk down the stairs that weren't there, called, "That's the short cut."

How Indians (usually the older men) can squat for what appears as an interminable length of time was a source of amazement. Furthermore, it is quite astounding how in a land of accepted dirtiness, how clean the people intend to be: the leaf brooms that sweep the stretch of sidewalk adjacent to their homes and /or shops; the daily laundry chore of beating clothing upon rocks in a running source of water (a river or a stream); the ritual of street morning bathing with a pan full of water, or in pools of rain (Calcutta). This includes finger brushing of teeth. I know it is hard to believe in a hot climate, but body odor was notable by its absence—even in a crowded bus load of people. As an aside, men's handkerchiefs are probably more widely used for mopping perspiration from face and neck than for blowing the nose.

Market areas throughout the country are truly a fascination! In some areas (Panjim) the shops close during the hot afternoon. Often in one particular street area can be grouped nothing but household wares (brass pots) or tailors and clothing shops, or chemists, or food stalls. Others may exhibit a hodge-podge of shops.

With such a huge population to be served, probably every shopkeeper ekes out some type of living. Serving the public on the street by cleaning the ears, barbering, shaving, shoe repairing, shoe shining is a very common sight. The mounds of prepared food (often swarming with flies) must at some point of time by late evening be consumed by the hordes of street walkers. And restaurants, more often than not, are very crowded.

And not to be overlooked in tourist areas, are the street vendors, often young children, selling knick-knacks. Hearing 'Frere Jacques, Frere Jacques'| sung and played on small, home-crafted fiddles eventually became very monotonous in the Jaisalmer area. Or the older women who firmly grasp the arms of "old" people descending from ferries, chanting, "Very dangerous, very dangerous" and then demand a fee for their services or the boys on airport buses who grab suitcases and then hold out their hands for money. Very enterprising!

Adding a few general observations: this may be a remaining custom of English rule: the varied uniforms, particularly hats of policemen in different states, the often brightly colored uniformed hotel and restaurant doormen. Depending with whom one spoke, the older people felt the India under English rule was far superior to the present, while the younger generation believed the new India to be greater.

The whole of India would come to a standstill if a shortage of carbon paper developed!

Certainly India is no different from many western nations, but punctuality is not one of peoples' fortes.

The sharing of a room in the house or sidewalk with cows or beasts of burden is the accepted thing. But at the same time, the manner in which many of these beasts are usually so heavily loaded is unbelievable. Mention can also be made of the gathering of fresh cow dung with bare hands and then left to dry for fuel chips.

Further interesting facets were the custom of eating, even sloppy foods, mixed with rice, with the fingers (the reason for a tap and sink in most restaurants to wash one's hands). In the Darjeeling area tea was often poured into a saucer and slurped from there. The art of drinking from a common container without touching it to one's lips, simply pouring it down one's throat amazed me.

I grew to enjoy much of India's spicy foods (except curry) much more than I ever dreamed possible. Even if onions are far from my favorite vegetable, my first choice had to be Tandoori chicken with nan (flat bread). However, in Kashmir, the increased spiciness was a little more than I could handle. I enjoyed mutton and paneer (cheese) dishes. Ice cream (particularly mango and pista) I ate with abandon, but many confections were overwhelmingly sweet.

I thrilled to a couple Indian cultural performances worthy of mention: the Kathakali dancing in Ernamkulam with its stories told through body, eye and hand movements; in Bombay the concert that presented instrumental music (sitars and tablas), the notable Sint. Gangubai Hangal whose wide voice range, powerful, forceful, had all the listeners spellbound, and a barefooted folk-dancer her ability amplified with belled ankles.

From snotty-nosed kids (particularly in the north) to the aged, many deceptively older looking than actual age; from the small-boned, short in stature, average Indian man to the tall, powerful, turbaned Sikhs; from the vendor who will cheat the tourist who appears to have a never-ending supply of money, to Mother Teresa, humble, benevolent, whom I met personally in Calcutta; I repeat, India is a land of extremes. And with these contrasts, deep, intense, enchanting, India creates an aura of magic. I am still within her spell!

THIS IS INDIA-1991

India's aura and mystique that prevailed for me travelling solo for eight weeks in 1989 were encroached by more realistic vistas in the six weeks (November-December) of travelling with a companion.

One of the greatest attractions, the people, remained the same. As in many other countries in the world, the tourist, the different-coloured skin, the likely affluent, is the recipient of various dispositions: friendliness, courtesy, graciousness, honesty and the contrasts, dishonesty, rudeness, "laissez-faire", "no problem" when often there was.

My (our) friends, Sheroo, Rusi, Anaheeta, Vispi in Bombay and Adil in Bangalore, were each the epitome of gracious hosts, wonderful ambassadors for their country! When my pre-planning for hotel accommodation in Bombay did not materialize (the YMCA does not accept credit cards), Anaheeta, despite being a new mother of one-month old Kizene, made certain we secured hotel accommodation! Her chauffeur, Harri, drove us to various sights (sites) around the city the next day. And how many delicious meals, prepared by their houseboy, did we share with Sheroo and Rusi? And Vispi, who with Rusi, took us sailing in the harbour—a first of me, the land-lubber!

Busy (and always hungry?) Adil found time in both Bombay and Bangalore to feed us well: mango milk shakes, kulki cones, snacks of chips, spicy tandoori chicken, and the truly "piece de resistance": a serving of FOUR filet mignon steaks each in a crowded indoor-outdoor Indian restaurant. Excellent fare! But how does one justify not eating it all when there is a multitude of people hungry?

We also met again vivacious, friendly Lyaqueet, the twelve year old artist (who isn't one?) in Udaipur. He had the inside track when I bought another oil on silk painting. We learned he was fortunate to have been befriended by an Austrian film maker and had spent a month in Vienna in the summer.

Roy, the waiter at Surya Sumudra, the romantic hideaway near Kovalum Beach, also had experienced life outside India. He had spent time in Italy with the manager, Klaus, a one-time German literature professor in Madras.

During our three day sojourn at Surya Sumudra, we encountered a variety of people: the enterprising fisherman, who for 100 rupees wished us to go out on the sea on his "boat", four or five poles lashed together; the quiet tillers of land who watched us trespass, but gave directions if we asked; the funeral group who willingly granted my request for pictures; in contrast, the father who for a fee, offered his children as camera subjects; the three guys who spoke no English, but commandeered us, my arm grimly grasped, and led us to Kovalum, probably a thirty minute walk; the little eight-year old Fatima who willingly went out of her way to show us the short cut to the beach—it was she who received the tip; the masseur (another first for me) who charged one-third the price asked at Culva Beach, Goa.

Yes, association with tourists generally means remuneration—and so much more than if performing the same task for natives; the watch repair man in Bombay who charged 125 rupees, only to have the watch quit again after twenty-four hours but in Trivandrum another repair man, pinpointing the problem, charged 60 rupees; the taxi driver at Bombay airport, despite having received the prepaid voucher, whined and wailed a sad tale, even before getting into the driver's seat; yet in Puna, our rickshaw driver who had been so patient after a long, hot day of sight-seeing and had been tipped generously, did not want to take any money to drive us to the train station next morning; the day tour guide in Goa who spoke little English, yet made a point of asking for a tip; the excellent guide and driver, very unassuming, on the three day trip to Ooty were most accommodating and most worthy of gratuities. (We've had a laugh about the Hong Kong currency mixed in with my friend's wallet and the quizzical looks Tom received when he unknowingly tried to dispense it in India!)

We could cite many examples of friendliness: The Bombay bankteller who restored Tom's faith in humanity after the horrific first night; the young man who spoke no English, but willingly walked to the chemists with us in Ooty; the temple policeman in Trivandrum who after he'd taken me to the sandalwood carving shop on the temple grounds, arranged for us to return that evening for our own guided tour up and down several streets to view, outside the Brahmin homes, the lighted coconut oil lamps, some very large and fancy, Such an experience he wished to share with us!

The onlookers tried to explain the strange phenomenon on the beach in Puri when hundreds of fish were being swept in with each incoming wave by wading out with long nets or simply kicking them from returning with the outgoing wave. How many fish were offered to us! Mystifying! An unbelievable fantastic sight that early evening. I can only think that God provided for the hungry!

The tourist sites, particularly the temple areas, and we visited quite a few, certainly were income sources for those who spoke English or in Udaipur, French and German. In Konarch, the temple to the Sun God and a World Heritage site, we enjoyed the explanation of monogamy, polygamy and polyandry, and having the erotica, some of which we likely would have missed ourselves, pointed out. Can you blame the man, hired at thirty-five rupees an hour, stretching the tour to two hours?

Such also was the situation on our early morning (6:00) leisurely boat ride on the Ganges in Varanasi. The funeral pyres, supposedly the most engaging sight, are the last to be viewed. We can't make it in the hour bargained. We can't turn around now! Nothing but necessary to pay an extra fifty rupees. But the sights here: people bathing, dipping, swimming, the crematorium spewing forth smoke, the piles of wood for the pyres, the measuring sticks for registering flood heights during monsoons, and even playful dolphins, were worth the cool excursion.

Also in Varanasi when our regular booked guide was late, the driver departed without him, in order to try to beat the curfew. At the Durga Temple, a sixteen year old boy, who looked more like ten, hopped in the car and took over the guide's duties. Did a fine job, too!

Monetarily, we would have been further ahead to have given a volunteering child two rupees to lead us to the library from which to view the Hindu Jagannath Temple in Puri. One of the most visited temples in India it is off-bounds for non-Hindus. Instead, when a bystander in an oil lamp shop offered to show us, we subjected ourselves, albeit interesting enough, to a Brahmin's view of matters and then he asked for a donation for temple work.

In some temples, after removing one's shoes and then retrieved for a small fee, one was free to gaze and no attempt to charge was ever made. In others, for example, Susheendram Temple near Kanniyakumari (Cape Cormorin) after Tom received the whole treatment of sandalwood paste and red kumkum on his forehead, chest and arms we were allowed to view fascinating things: a large Nandi (bull), created from seashell powder, a series of fourteen hollowed stone pipes that produced musical tones when tapped, a three hundred seventy year old tree growing through the roof, we willingly produced money.

We added to our education in Mt. Abu at the Palace Hotel, a former maharaja summer palace, the gardens of which have gone to ruin, unfortunately. The hotel clerk played upon our sympathies by stating he made but seven hundred rupees (thirty-five dollars) a month—and he had a B.A. We tipped all the staff, only to find when checking out that a ten percent service charge was added. That ploy has worked more than once, no doubt.

But Mt. Abu, that noted honeymoon area, despite a persistent beggar woman who sought us every day, was well worth the long bus ride from Udaipur and back. So many pleasant memories: the fantastically carved marble showcase of the Jain Dilwara Temple, the hidden Hindu temple in a cleft of stones requiring three hundred eighty steps to reach it., the colourfully lit Lake Nikki night scene, the delight of dressing in Rajastani costumes and being recorded on film for an exceptionally low fee, the joy of happening upon an outdoor school assembly recital and being invited to sit with the VIP's, if we wished.

And singing: on the bus ride back to Udaipur we heard both group and individuals accompanied by a mouth organ. Such gaiety! We learned that the chanting we listened to a number of nights was for a deceased Muslim, the body of which was wrapped in a sheet and deposited directly into the grave.

We were quite perturbed in both Varanasi and Udaipur when large tours (Japanese and Dutch) received the royal treatment in the restaurant and we had to seek waiters' attention. But the gratuities would have been much greater from the tours.

Yet another irksome aspect: in Varanasi we were taken to a silk shop by our guide and driver the first morning. There was no really high pressure salesmanship (a welcome change). But we decided to order matching cream silk shirts, made to measure. They were delivered to our hotel that evening but both had "black marks" and neither fit that well. These faults were to be remedied and before 8:30 next morning another man returned them. The marks were still partially visible and Tom's shirt was still too broad across the shoulders. It took some hassling but we had our money refunded. In contrast, my figured silk blouse, also tailor made, turned out to be quite acceptable. The prices here, in a government shop, were set; all the more reason to expect fine workmanship!

But bargaining is certainly a way of life for the tourist. We thought we had negotiated a reasonably fair deal on silver chains from an Udaipur merchant, until suddenly off the street came a guy who stated ten percent discount was too much; five percent is what it should be, We walked away. Vishnu, Bodhisattva, whomever, was looking after us. For, later, we were able to purchase chains for half the price from a merchant who spoke very little English.

I being the more experienced, bargained for taxi tours, but when the service was good, and generally it was, the original asking price was usually given. The trip was never too rapid; top speed was lucky to be seventy kilometers an hour before having to brake for some more cows or herd of goats, a cyclist or ten, dozens of pedestrians, or a vehicle of some size, be it bus, truck, car, rickshaw, motorbike, or some animal drawn cart.

(As an aside, we witnessed a cow run over by a camel drawn cart in Udaipur.) But at least in a taxi we avoided the "deluxe" or "luxury" buses, the impossible discards from goodness knows what other countries. All we had to do was accustom ourselves to the cacophony of horns! If nothing else works on a vehicle, the horns and brakes must!

To cover the vast distances we relied upon Indian Airlines, more often than not, late in departing. Thankfully, our one encounter with Indian trains (Bombay-Puna return) was not quite as frightful as my trip from Agra to New Delhi in 1989.

I might comment here on the custom officers at Bombay's International airport. Despite all the toughness on the surface, a couple of them at least have a sense of humour. Our small backpack was missing upon our arrival and after reporting it, we received a form. When we returned two days later, we could not find the form. Finally they decided if they could examine the contents thoroughly, we might be able to take the bag without the form. But the finding airline had sealed the zippers. Such a project to open them! Ultimately the man handed over a stamped card, grinned broadly and said, "TAKE IT—AND GO!"

Some progress is being made in the communications area. At least in Bombay, STD phone centres are being established. Those in charge are most helpful. It is no longer necessary to wait for hours in the post office to make an overseas call. And it is to be hoped that soon hotels will no longer charge for calls that are not completed or when the party is cut off.

We were fortunate to visit India at the time of Divali, the festival celebrating the conclusion of the monsoons. The marigold bouquets had special significance, as did the powdered decorations before doorways or on streets. But what we truly experienced was the Indians' exuberance in the nightly fireworks displays. We sat out on our balcony and thoroughly enjoyed what they offered.

Even Tom has had to concede that India has a special fascination. Perhaps unexplicable, but unfathomable or not, it is unmistakingly present. I still believe it is the people, as I have tried to exemplify. Yet—yet—can one dismiss the captivation, the bewilderment of the antiquity of so much of the country, its practices, its religions, its ethics?

THIS IS INDIA - 1995

Because my friend, Tom, and I had been in other Asiatic countries to begin our trip, this time we flew into Madras, rather than Bombay. We stayed in an airport hotel to begin. The room was damp and musty smelling and of course there was the usual moth balls scattered in the bathroom. Finally a travel agent was able to procure an inner city hotel for us. Hotels seemed to be hard to come by, if one did not have a reservation. It is strange how one, despite previous visits, has to accustom oneself to the sights, smells and the culture shock!

It all started when we were to board the plane in Kuala Lumpur, Malaysia. There happened to be a great many Indians who were returning home. Usually when one boards a plane, people with children, are given first priority. As soon as this message was given that such people could board, there was a mad rush to the desk, whether they had children or not! However, the airline did check that some of the large bags did not go aboard.

Our city tour, by taxi began with a Catholic church on the beach. It was interesting but the beggars were annoying! Then we viewed a musical fountain area being built with a huge, white statue of Bodhisattva, tanks of tropical fish and cages of birds. However, thoughtfully, the guys in charge started up the fountain and lights for us when it is usually an evening program. (I have not been back to Madras or Chennai as it is now known to view the finished product.) After lunch we stopped at a fishing "port" and bridge and also an archeological site with huge rocks. Late afternoon I took a walk along the long thirteen kilometer beach (the one Keith, the young hotel worker had taken me in 1989). Had to dodge the vendors of this and that, but I did have some Canadian coins for a young boy who very politely said, "Thank you."

The next day was spent driving over terrible roads to Kanchipuram noted for its seaside temples. The first we saw were a long series of temples carved out of the rock. The balancing rock was also worthy of viewing. Hawkers and guys wishing to be guides were overwhelming. One of the most important temples, Kamakashiamman is dedicated to Shiva and apparently at the full moon in March hundreds of couples decide to be married. Among the others, Ekamhareshwara and Kailasenatha we also viewed Pallava, another seventh century one being restored. There were quite a number of inside painted areas that were still visible. Evidently when the English were there they had much of the original sandstone pillars and carvings done over with plaster. The cherished elephant was carved in the entrance to one temple. (That is one reason that in the tourist shops one finds all sizes and materials of elephants. Also why the artists in Udaipur, seem to concentrate on painting elephants. Three of the five pictures I have bought in Udaipur over the years are of elephants!)

I must not forget at one outdoor breakfast that the crows were very brazen. One, in fact, swooped down and took something off Tom's plate! Greyish crows and green parrots were most prevalent.

If one thing was economical, food was. Breakfast was usually included with the price of a hotel. We had some absolutely delicious prawns before we got back into Madras that evening.

We left the rain (off and on) and flew the short distance to Bangalore—even so Indian airlines was ninety minutes late. We met Kashmin, Adil's selected wife, and little Edul, a beautiful baby with big brown eyes. One day they drove us into the country to their club where the men swam. Also learned that Kashmin, who incidentally has her PhD from an English university, is a wonderful cook and is also adept at needlepoint.

Each time I have been to Bangalore, I have bought sandals., so reasonable in price for the fine quality. Tom also bought some loafers that what would have cost well over one hundred dollars back in Canada for less than half that price.

This is true if one buys a book published in India. It is quite economical whereas if one buys out of the country published book, it is high-priced.

I might mention that this was still before email and ATM's in India. It was necessary to send post cards home and to use traveller's cheques for cash. Using a credit card often meant a five percent surcharge. As always one had to check the rates of exchange of the numerous money changers. Going into a bank usually took ages to make a transaction.

After having to identify our bags on the tarmac, we took a small plane to Madurai—soon to become my favourite sites in India because of its Meenanski temple,

elaborately ornate, and so colourful. Awesome was its height with a strange creature atop to ward off the evil spirits. It was constructed in 1560, according to my notes. We did not have the best of hotels and we often left it to gaze again at the temple. (As an aside it was here also for our lunch that we bought tomatoes that were so fresh and juicy—so different from those we have imported to Western Canada. And they were so economical!)

After checking prices and bargaining (I am pretty good at it), we moved onto Kodaikanal, one of the famous English hill stations. Not too far from Madurai we stopped to view the Tirumalai Nayak Palace built in 1636. Its huge pillars and golden throne made the stop worthwhile. Aboard a mini van we wound up and up with a stop at an interesting museum en route. We learned that the brown crested birds we had witnessed in Madras were Ceylon Coupees. The stop at the Viraganur dam wasn't worth the parking fee. However the next stop was a Hindu temple, Thirupparankundram, built into the side of a rock and swarming with Hindus come to worship for the holiday Pongal, the time in January that the sun begins northwards. I know Shiva and the bull Nandi were involved also. The number of times I have been to India I still cannot differentiate among the many gods and goddesses!

Despite the misty rain in the days we were there, we walked around the lake a number of times. Each time we would meet Indians who wanted to have their picture taken with us. I do not think it was the misty fog that may have made many men think they could urinate anywhere along the lake. I stated that if I even had one rupee for each man I saw urinating, I would be rich!

We also visited Bryant's Park, noted for its rose garden, but in January there were not too many blossoms.

With some mix-up as to pick-up to go back to Madurai,(I got a refund when I checked the office in Madurai) we had to take a private car. It was fine until after twilight (and thankfully out of the curves) that our driver decided to not use his head lights unless he had the vision to see another vehicle approaching. A frightening half hour or so!

We had booked the train to Trivandrum with an agent in Kodi but when we checked at the station in Madurai there was no record of our reservation. Fortunately there was space. I can still hear Tom saying when he looked into our designated car," This is first class??" It was far from luxurious! However, even on an overnight train, the fans whirring above us were welcome! In the early morning we noted we were passing through coconut and banana plantations.

We liked Trivandrum from our 1991 trip, but the hotel room we procured (no reservation) was on the first floor overlooking a busy street. Noise!! It bears repeating: horns honking continuously. We arrived on a Sunday and the city shops were mostly closed. Monday we found the tourist information and they were able to get us a reservation at Surya Sumudra again. It was expensive but so peaceful. And the mussels were so delicious, as were the other meals!! Because of the price we were ready to fly to Sri Lanka early, but Klaus decided to give us a fifty percent discount. We stayed four days!

The last day was very interesting in that repairs on the swimming pool had begun. There was quite the assembly line:workers passing along trays of cement for the bottom of the pool; others passing empties back; a couple carrying pails of water; some mixing with long-handled hoes the cement; women in saris carrying in the bags of cement on their heads. And all this in the heat of the day!

During the late afternoon I went for a walk along the road and was greeting people I met. One teen-aged girl took me by surprise when I answered her question as to how I was. I said I was fine and asked how she was. Her answer was. "Happy." It brought tears to my eyes. It seems they have so little and yet are quite content with their lot.

THIS IS INDIA—2001

Back in India once again—it does seem to have a calling! We flew into Madras again and then to Bangalore. We met a couple at a restaurant who even with three children of their own were adopting an Indian child. Their first impression of India was described as being one of wonderment and disbelief.

Adil has coined the phrase Might is Right. The larger the vehicle the more right one has on the road! Without a doubt there is a pecking order. The horns are always blaring, but at the same time there is an acceptance of politeness. It is not unusual to see a vehicle going the wrong way on a one-way street or highway. (One still sees this.)

By now Adil and Kashmin have added another son, Cyrus, now in play school. Such well behaved children. As Adil is a priest in their Parsee religion, so shall each of these boys be priests.

One night when they had finally allowed us to pay for dinner and wine (the latter that is beginning to improve in quality over the years,) at our hotel, they phoned from the lobby to come see the beginning of a Hindu wedding. We did not see the bride anywhere but the bridegroom, colourfully and elaborately dressed was seated upon a horse and surrounded by a huge crowd of guys.

Although there seemed to be a few ATM's in Madras and Bangalore, it was difficult to find one that would accept our debit cards. I finally found one that took my card and I no longer had to rely on travellers cheques.

Although he had to pay extra for using his credit card, for my up-coming birthday, Tom bought me a 22K gold chain bracelet for two hundred Canadian. What is it worth today? After reading in the paper how gangs of young boys were snatching gold jewellery from people's necks, I made certain my new bracelet remained safe!

On this trip Adil and Kashmin and boys drove us to the Nandihills where from the height we had quite the view. All the Indians in their Sunday finery were in their usual jovial picnic mood! We ended up at their club again for a swim. Also one evening before dinner we walked around the perimeter of the parliament building.

Tom, I have to add now, was originally from England and knew all about cricket. I, a Canadian, knew nothing about the game. In our leisure time in a hotel Tom liked to watch cricket and began to tell me what the game was all about. I became enamoured with young Sachin Tandulhar, who actually began Test matches when he was but sixteen years old and is now nearing thirty-nine years of age. Still playing, he is a cricketer, most worshipped in the world!

Before we headed south we flew to Udaipur, one of my favourite cities in India. It was great to go through the rambling city palace again. Although it would have been nice to have stayed in the Lake Palace Hotel, beautiful and exotic, it was beyond our budget and without a reservation we could not stay there as a walk-in. Instead we did take the small ferry across Lake Pichola and explored the environs.

It was a common occurrence, so I may mention from the hotel we did stay which overlooked a small stream, we could see men squatting for their morning constitutional.

I believe he spotted me first, although I was looking for the little boy from whom I had bought a painting in 1989. I bought two more from a teen-age boy now.

Our next port of call was Mt Abu, the honeymoon destination. The one thing that stands out for me is the beautifully carved (chiselled) Jain temple—simply stunning. (Jains evidently do not kill anything, not even an insect!) Tom and I, although not married, had our picture take in the regalia of the Indians.

(Tom's grandson thought it was hilarious when he saw it.) I do not recall the bus ride there, but the bus ride from there had a group of Indians, fun-loving and almost boisterous. They sang almost all the way home. I loved them! Often they are a frolicsome people!

En route by car from Bangalore to Cochin, we stopped at a small town overnight. The so-called manager of the hotel asked, after dinner, if he could come to our room and talk. What he had in mind was how he might be able to be sponsored to come to Canada. We exchanged email addresses, even though neither Tom nor I knew the ins and out of the process. Next morning, even though he had desk clerks using computers, he decided to do the calculations of our stay himself without using a computer. I had to ask for a receipt and it was only when we were loaded into the car that I thought we had been overcharged by five hundred rupees. When I went back to check, he said the cash we had given him was correct. It was his word against ours—he could have already stashed away the five hundred rupees. This has given me the opinion that the Indians will not rob you, but they will cheat you!

One thing I wanted to do in Cochin was to return to St Francis church where Vasco da Gama was buried until his remains were moved to Lisbon. But these rickshaw drivers want to take you to shops first (although I have no proof of it, I believe they receive a commission on the merchandise a tourist might buy.) We also witnessed the fishermen perched on a pole in the sea. As well there were large container ships being loaded.

Here, also we arranged our next stops. First stop was inland at Spice Village, Kumily. It took us five hours by car over rough roads, full of pot-holes. The road construction was almost laughable. Two flagmen with red and green flags to stop and proceed and rickshaws with a box that held the tarred pebbling received from a larger truck.

The scenery, once we reached the Western Ghat Mountains was quite spectacular. We viewed rubber plantations, tea and coffee plantations and a number of flowering trees. The tapping of the rubber trees with shades of different types were particularly interesting. In the late afternoon we boarded a hotel sponsored boat on Periyar Lake where we viewed various flora and fauna. The colourful blue-green kingfishers were a treat as were the large (compared to our Canadian ones) playful otters. We saw a lot of cormorants, particularly in their nesting trees, a darter and both grey and white herons. Elephants seemed quite prolific: we saw one herd of twelve with three babies. As well a large group of wild boars, gaurs and sambars were pointed out. (Unfortunately my camera had stopped working and I could not buy another in India with a zoom lens; I had to wait until I returned to Singapore to purchase one.)

That evening we and three tour buses were treated to a musical presentation of a guy singing with his accompanists, followed by a male and a female dancer, the latter who was very agile and expressive.

From all that we had witnessed, one would have thought we had found a wonderful place. However, our cottage was very crude. To top matters off, when we returned that evening, there was no power. Somehow a main switch inside had been hit. We had to console ourselves that "This is India".

Next morning we were ready to move onto our next destination, the Coconut Lagoon, but a phone call revealed they could not accommodate us until the next day as we had booked. I booked a massage. (In the massages I have had in India, they do not partially cover you or ask you to leave your panties on; one is massaged naked. What is wrong with that? Nothing. They use oil, not lotion, as well, and then wipe you down with water and a cloth.) For a seventy-five minute massage it cost me approximately ten dollars Canadian.

Later that morning our driver took us to a spice plantation tour. We walked for over an hour as the guide explained very carefully all the leaves, fruits (beans) and roots of a great many bushes and trees: two different coffees, tea, tiny red chilies (hot), ginger, vanilla, cardamom, nutmeg, cinnamon, allspice, cloves, as well as teak, betel and banana. To top it off we saw three different species of birds we had not seen before: a bulbul, a couple of tiny sunbirds and a long wavy tailed blackbird. Our driver met us at the end so that we did not have to retrace our steps. Then we were taken to the owner's house where his wife ground up with mortar and pestle some spices to make us some marsala tea. I wasn't too impressed, but it was an experience.

That afternoon to satisfy our driver we were driven to about four different shops. We did not want to buy spices, but did buy a large bag of cashews. After some dickering, I ended up buying a dainty turquoise and brown star-sapphire necklace. I also added a Buddha to my collection Here I might add that on my first visit to India Adil gave me a tiny Buddha that fit into my wallet. Unfortunately on one of our trips, my purse was stolen in Singapore and my tiny Buddha went with it! However, over the years of travelling (particularly in Asia) I have added a great many Buddhas of all shapes and materials: stones of various composition, wood, glass and metal. Some are cheap, others are expensive.) My collection is now nearing fifty.

As the wine in India left a lot to be desired, in order to keep Tom company for "sundowners", we began buying small bottles of rum—very inexpensive, approximately sixty-five cents Canadian!.

Once again it was hard to say goodbye to India!

THIS IS INDIA–2004

This trip to India involved a different route. We first flew to London where we visited friends and relatives. Then we deplaned in New Delhi. Tom was finally going to see some new parts of India and I was to re-visit areas I had first explored in 1989. Our first task was to contact my nephew who was also travelling in northern India at the same time. He came into New Delhi to spend one afternoon and dinner that evening with us. (He also was enjoying India.)

Our next undertaking was to contact a travel agent to arrange for a car and driver to conduct us around the circle. What a fine tour guide he proved to be! He would stop and explain aspects to us when and if we or he wished.

First part of first day was to see some of New Delhi. We saw the India Gate and the Ghandi statue, but without making notes, many of the other buildings became a blur to me.

Then it was off to Agra where Tom was to marvel at the edifice, Taj Mahal. Actually it is so well-known little can be said to describe it except it is a marvel of white marble with inlaid flowers, taking twenty-two years to build by Shah Jahan in memory of his wife.

Agra fort was on the itinerary as well. Here one can view the Taj Mahal at a distance. It also has some impressive buildings, the Divanl-Khas for one.

I rather remember Fatehpur Sikri as quite a small, but interesting area. I hardly recognized it as being the same area. It had grown considerably and there were hawkers and small shops galore.

A two-day stop we made was Ranthambore National Park where tigers still reside. Despite going out in their jeeps twice a day, we did not see a trace of a tiger. There was a young couple who were going to stay a third day. I have often wondered if they were successful in spying a tiger?

Our driver stopped beside the road one morning to talk to some migrants who had camped in the ditch. The women were gaudily dressed but had wide silver bracelets on their arms. They even let me take a photo without asking for rupees! An interesting aspect also was that there were twin babies who had been born just 6 days before. What a life!!

Another unscheduled stop was at Lampali school. I spotted kids playing in the school yard and asked the driver to stop so I might take a photo. Someone in authority spotted me and invited both Tom and me to be their guests on the platform that had been set up for their program that was to celebrate Republic Day. We were adorned with marigold wreaths and eventually given (albeit crude) a trophy marking the occasion. I still have it among my Indian collection (white Buddhist scarves, a yellow head covering from Amtritsar, among other things). Indeed we were treated as VIP's. Their program consisted of outdoor races of different sorts and then on stage, several girls in their native finery performed various dances. At the conclusion both Tom and I were asked to say a few words. The majority of the kids did not understand a word we said, I am certain, but the teachers on stage with us did understand English. However there was one boy who gave a speech in English stating the aspects, worthy and superior, of living in India. He spoke of how proud he was to be an Indian! As a former school teacher, I thoroughly enjoyed the morning!)

Our driver had us staying in former maharajas' palaces and havelis that had been converted into hotels.

The havelis were previous merchant houses on the Silk Road. Some were still in very fine condition while others were sadly near ruins. One bathroom really amused us. One had to walk up five or six steps to reach the toilet. Is that where the expression "sitting on the throne" was coined?

Of course, we had to return to Udaipur before carrying on to Pushkar.

This was my first visit to this town and it truly surprised me! There are a number of large temples and the lake itself is worthy of a visit. On toward Bikaner where just outside the town we stopped at the Karni Mata Temple which has rats and more rats running around. It is the rats' temple and they are fed and cared for there. Not certain, I appreciated a rat or six running over my feet, but we were taken there to see the place. If one sees the while albino rat it is supposed to mean good luck. We saw it feeding with some others.

Then it was on to Jodhpur, known as the "blue city" because the buildings, for the most part are painted blue. The impressive fort and museum were worth the visit. However, I do not think it measures up, in my opinion to the City Palace and its museum in Jaipur, "the pink city" thus named because of the pink-coloured sandstone constructions. Perched high on a hill also, heavily decorated elephants prepare, for a fee, to take tourists to the top. Tom and I rode one up, but walked down. I recall the beautiful windows within.

Before returning us to New Delhi, our driver asked if we would like to visit his sister's house. She was one of the better income class and had a house, most trim and neat. I do not believe we were expected but it did not take long for the neighbours' curiosity to prevail! Soon we were gazed upon by total strangers, listening to the conversation.

To complete this road tour we flew to Bangalore for a weekend visit with Adil and Kashmin and boys, such wonderful friends.

Another trip to Madurai, but this time instead of simply marvelling at the colours of the front, we somehow learned that we could wander around back and enter into the vast temple. All the many visits there we had never done anything but gaze at its front splendour. We traveled to Cochin again before reaching Trivandrum where we then flew to Sri Lanka. But before departing I spotted these boys. Do you not love the smile on the one in front?

THIS IS INDIA-2007

2004 was to be Tom's last visit to India as he died in 2006.

When I received an invitation from Kashmin to attend her niece's thread ceremony in Ahmedabad, a city I had not visited, I asked my unmarried son if he might like to go to India. His first response was that he would have to think about it. But eventually the answer was positive and we applied for our visas.

Before reaching Bangalore, we visited Hong Kong, Brunei and Borneo. Because it was a busy time of the year and hotels are expensive we were given rooms in a club. Not the greatest but there was one older man who befriended us. A travel agent arranged for us to go south of Mysore to Nagarahole National Park. We rode through the jungle by jeep until we reached a lake where we boarded big saucer-like coracle boats. We saw an elephant and several cute spotted deer. It was a birders paradise as well with blue kingfishers, egrets, and cormorants, It was so calm and serene, But no elusive tigers! On our return we stopped for a tour of Mysore Palace. The value of the silver and gold must be tremendous! We admired greatly the carved teak doors, ceilings and domes.

Back at Bangalore we saw the travel agent again to prepare for the next journey.

Kashmin also took me shopping. But with the rupee worth about $.025 now, it is still not expensive to shop—especially in Bangalore. We also had a delicious pom-frit fish dinner along with some good wine (made in India—how the wine has improved from the sweet Goa wine that was all that was available for many years.) Showing their kindness and generosity, I was given a diamond pendant, but I was to look for a chain that would fit through the small loop.

I had undergone a police check and received permission to visit a boy, Mahesh, and his family, whom I sponsored through World Vision. A World Vision employee drove me to a small village outside Hyderabad city and then acted as an interpreter. Mahesh, in the eighth grade was willing to have his photo taken with me, but he would not smile. Yet when he was excited about something and speaking in his language he had a beautiful smile. As could be expected, practically the entire village came to visit. The family, who lived in a dirt-floored house (and

I never saw any beds) provided everyone with bought cookies and orange tang. (I never thought to refuse the latter but I did not suffer from Delly Belly.) Of course I was greeted with marigold lais—four of them in fact. They became quite heavy and was glad when I could dispose of them back at the hotel.

I was taken a short distance to the play school where a teacher and ONE assistant handled forty children. Did they ever deserve a medal! Passing by we saw an igloo shaped pen with kids (baby goats) that were so cute.

That evening Don and I wandered away from the hotel to find a restaurant. (We actually found our way back much better than the taxi driver who took us there from the airport. He had to ask about three different people before he found it.) Across from us at dinner were two business men, one of whom was Indian. They ordered a bottle of wine and offered some to us. We did not refuse! When a second bottle was ordered, again we were offered another glass. Being on an expense account helps!

The next day when we thought we were going to sight see but found the price for foreigners was ten times as much as for natives, we decided to simply walk around the markets.

Our next destination was Bhubaneshwar, where after a five hour layover in Chenin and two hour delay, we were greeted with marigold leis and our picture taken. Next morning the taxi driver showed us our picture in the paper, caption in Hindi. VIP's!

Although it was a nice enough hotel, we had a great deal of trouble getting much warm water to shower in the morning. This is India (yet).

The morning was spent visiting temples. The first was a seventh century temple, followed by a ninth century temple. Next was an eleventh century complex of temples that non-Hindus are not allowed to enter. The last was a "dead" temple where an admission fee was required (the others had just been donations.) It might be mentioned that several erotic figures were carved into these temples. Even more so were erotic figures evident in the temple at Konark

But before Konark we visited second century Jain caves. I believe there were about thirty-seven of them remaining. They were not overly decorative, but they were interesting. There were several groups of Indians visiting there also and as usual, wanted to have their pictures taken with us! There were a multitude of monkeys in the area as well. Some people were feeding them peanuts. Have I mentioned that monkeys are not my favourite animal? From my travels I do not trust them!

Another interesting aspect at the caves was a "gravel tree." People who were having troubles in life, found a small stone, wrapped a piece of cloth around it and attached it to a branch of the tree. If you believe enough, it probably will happen. It made for a colourful display!

Next morning we were given a tour of Kolkata. We saw the white marble Victoria Monument with the statue of the queen constructed by the British. Many other British constructed edifices were pointed out. But what really took my attention was the Jain temple: chandeliers of crystal, Chinese vases and so much more! The afternoon was spent browsing markets and small malls. Our driver took us to a coffee shop where young and old gathered. He even bought us two small clay flower pots. But this visit, no Mother Teresa!

En route to the airport next morning, I did not note nearly as many people sleeping on the sidewalk as I had witnessed in 1989. But there were rats running about. Ugh!

Now I must mention that there are several small airlines to give Indian Airlines competition. Adil recommended Kingfisher. However, in our flight to New Delhi we somehow missed our flight even though they claimed to have called our names. However we were able to get seats on a later flight that afternoon. After a night spent at an airport hotel we were on our way to Amritsar.

The Sikh Golden Temple rivals, in my opinion, the Taj Mahal! It is open to all religions to worship. One must remove one's shoes and socks (common in most temples). The dome evidently has seven hundred fifty kilograms of gold and is a symbol of the Sikhs' way of living a pure life.. We visited with our Sikh guide the Martyrs area where evidently the British fired against the Sikhs in the 1920's. There were pictures of a few who resisted and they were generally hanged. Also viewed was the sculpture of the "flame of remembrance." I remember hearing about its destruction by the Indian army in 1984, but fortunately when I visited in 1989 it had been rebuilt.

Something I saw this time was the kitchen where evidently at least fifty thousand people are fed daily. There were huge cauldrons of rice and lentils and even an automatic chapati maker. Those being fed were seated cross-legged on the floor and of course eating with their hands.

That afternoon we searched the jewellery shops again as Don wanted a gold bracelet and I still had not found a chain for my diamond pendant. Guess what? We found both in the same shop.

We also inquired about the meeting of the Pakistani and Indian guards at the border crossing for that afternoon-evening. It turned out rather disappointing. There were bleachers set up but they were quite a distance from the border, per se. The Indian soldiers were dressed to the hilt and strutted with high steps and salutes in front of us several times as they marched to the "no man's area" and back. I thought the Pakistani guards would be coming to perform as well, but not so; we had to gaze at what they were doing at a distance in their country. Eventually, the Indian guards pompously strutted to the border where they met their counterparts to shake hands, to fold their respective flags and the border was officially closed for the night.

The next day (December 15) was my birthday and we were scheduled to fly back that morning to New Delhi and be picked up by a driver to take us to Agra. But this is India! Our flight was cancelled and we had to wait until late afternoon before departing. Fortunately an Indian woman who has been living in London, England for some time was a talkative and interesting person with whom to converse. Don had his sudoku puzzles.

When it was time to board, I mentioned it was my birthday and asked what the chances were of getting into business class. No problem and when we reached New Delhi the driver had two dozen roses for me from Kashmin and Adil and boys!! Such fine friends!

That evening the driver took us to the back side of the Taj Mahal and it was certainly a different view than any I had had before! But that was all I was to see of it this time as "Delly Belly" struck me during the night. (I should have known better than to have salad for dinner that evening.) Don took a guide and was very impressed with the Taj Mahal the next day.

It was a long journey to Jaipur especially with road construction. But here I might mention they have machines doing the work, not hand labour as it used to be!

We also stopped at Fatehpur Sikri and have changes been made there! Cars are not allowed to the top. One has to take a bus up to view the three palaces (and other buildings) that Akbar, a Mogal emperor in the 1500's, had constructed for his three wives. (We had earlier stopped at Akbar's tomb.) As well all the commercial shops were below!

Jaipur, the pink city, never disappoints! The same colourfully decorated elephants patiently trudge up and down the hill to the City Palace, which is still occupied by a former royal family. It is an immense building of which one is only able to view about one-tenth of it. As in most castles or palaces one sees the table settings, an art gallery, the armory, among other rooms. The afternoon was spent at a rug-weaving shop, a print shop and the planetarium (still under construction). Without a doubt, the rug weaving is an art. Only thing that bothers me is that often it is young boys who should be in school who are mastering the trade.

Once we left Kolkata we were housed in very fine accommodation: either a havali or a former maharaja's palace. That is until we flew into Udaipur where we had the tiniest of rooms, even if it did overlook the lake.

Whether he wished to stay ahead of larger groups, I felt the guide rushed us through Udaipur palace and the twice before I had been there, I had never had a guide to explain things. C'est la vie!

Next we were put on a little boat (no life jackets, of course) and taken around a lake. We had about ten or fifteen minutes on the island to view the summer palace that had nothing but an expensive restaurant. Next was the Royal Garden. Very nice palms and mangos were beheld. In summer I am certain it would be a beautiful area.

Later that afternoon I decided to wander around. I did not buy any art at this point, but did buy Kashmiri scarves for my sisters, daughter and myself. I also bought a sweater, but I do not think I got any real bargains.

Next day Don and I walked and walked, but I took time to have a haircut. It was very reasonably priced and I was pleased with it. Both of us ended up buying some art from a shop. When it was only twenty rupees more to have it framed, decided to buy a framed picture instead of bringing it home to pay so much more to have it done.

We finally reached Don's destination of the "Prince's" prestige cars. Water or a soft drink was included with the price of admission. A guide took us and a fellow from England around telling us about each car's features.

It was another short night before we had to board the train for Ahmedabad. Our cabin companions happened to be a pair of girls from the Netherlands and involved in medical research. They had done quite a bit of travelling and so we had a lot to discuss.

We arrived in Ahmedabad shortly after 4:00 and were taken to the hotel that used to belong to one of Kashmin's relatives. It was one of the nicest we had stayed. However, we received little sleep as Adil and Kashmin were in the rotunda at 8:30. Visited with them as we ate breakfast and then at 11:00 we were whisked away by an excellent Brahmin female guide for a city tour.

Gandhi's ashram which was his headquarters during his fight for India's independence was exceptionally interesting. Next we drove a distance out of the city to the Step Well, five storeys in depth. It was unbelievable how cool it was, even with the two wells often dry. There are several mosques in the city, and I do not know which one we stopped to visit. It was an enormous one! After four hours of touring and so little sleep, we begged off for the rest of the tour.

That evening Adil came to pick us up for the pre-celebrations at Kashmin's sister's apartment. Such an array of saris, colourful, devastatingly elegant and graceful! One slim girl who had just returned from England with a PhD was clad in a stunning silver sari! The jewellery worn by the ladies was also resplendent! They were all so friendly towards us. Food was served, but once again I have to state that as much as I love the Indian people, I am not fond of their food.

Because Adil thought it best for Don and me to fly to Mumbai the evening of the thread ceremony so we might not miss our flight to Singapore the following morning, the ceremony itself was held in the morning—to accommodate us!

Held outdoors on a platform, Adil and his two sons wore their priestly garments, but it was the resident priest who actually conducted the ceremony. I learned that they wear this thread and a shirt all the time except for bathing.

I have to confess afterwards my attention switched to that of one young boy and his father who were playing cricket with the small boy the bowler—so comical and so cute!

When we arrived at the international airport in Mumbai I could not believe the shiny modern building, contrast to the dreary, drab one of years ago!

THIS IS INDIA—2011

I guess India gets in one's blood. When I asked my son if he would like to return to India again, he did not hesitate long in responding yes. It was I who was about to back out when it was absolutely necessary to apply for visas on-line. Such a problem I had, but eventually I persevered.

Having visited a lot of the north four years ago, I suggested we choose the south this trip. I actually had in mind some resorts Tom and I had visited, but Don rebelled, "I want to see things!"

He had not seen any of Mumbai, so we flew into that city. I had booked a hotel quite close to the city centre and they had taken the funds from my credit card. However, when we arrived, they could find no record of my reservation. (This is India!) They had a room they could put us in on the second floor. Next morning, the manager was very apologetic saying I had booked a superior room and we were moved to the ninth floor with a sea view.

Although we were close by the Gate of India, it was impossible to approach too near as it was Navy Day and it was blocked off. That evening the crowds to see the navy perform were unreal! We wandered around the Taj Mahal Hotel and then went to the Prince Albert Museum, now renamed Chhatrapati Shivaji Maharaj Vastu Sangrahalaya. (Only the natives can pronounce it; it will always be the Prince Albert Museum for me.) It is a vast building that houses items from all over India.

Next day we took a four hour tour of the city, but because we had been to the museum it turned out to be only three hours. I was truly amazed at the new hospital, decoratively domed. We could not stop any length of time at the Jain Temple as parking was at a premium. We were able to stretch our legs at the hanging gardens. We viewed where all the washing is done and then spread out on the grass to dry in the hot sun. As we had driven along "the necklace", the curved road leading into the city proper en route to the hotel that first night, we did not really need to see it in daylight. When our driver asked if there was something else we wanted to see, I suggested the Thieves Market, but was told it was hard to park in that area.

We spent time with a travel agent booking our flight to Kochi, only to find that we were booked in an airport hotel that really smelled musty! (Again this is India!) However, we met with the congenial manager who cheerfully arranged to transfer us to a sister hotel in the city (It smelled much better.)

Next morning a rickshaw driver wished to take us to Kochi (we were in Erakulum. What a hot and exhaust-filled morning! We crossed over the new bridge (the two English constructed ones are still there). I was so disappointed in the St Francis Church which I had seen so white and pristine. We could not go into it as there was scaffolding all around; I hope they were preparing to repaint it as it was really dingy. Vasco da Gama was buried there for fourteen years before his body was taken to Lisbon. We viewed the enormous Catholic Basilica before starting the homeward journey. As always, fruit and vegetable markets, so fresh, so colourful, are in evidence.

The rickshaw operator knew of a travel agency and took us there to arrange our journey to Bangalore where we were to arrive on the twentieth of December. We ended up with a driver, excellent and accommodating, by the name of Vanesh. Whereas we were to spend two days in each of the towns we visited and figured Vanesh would let us be on our own the second day, he had arranged always something for us to see or do the second day.

Before we left our Kochi hotel, I decided to have an ayurvedic treatment, hoping it might alleviate the pain in my left calf that has bothered for ages and for which I have had various treatments here in Canada. Two girls oiled me down and massaged me before showering me like a child. The price was reasonable, but unfortunately it did not help. Neither did two other treatments that I had during our voyage help. I am just going to have to live with the pain that seems to come and go.

Our first stop was at Monnar, a new area for me. En route we viewed several crops: coffee, black pepper, tea, cocoa, cardamom, pineapple, tapioca. One of the most interesting aspects was the rubber plantations with the trees tapped and dripping into cups. Then we saw the latex hanging and drying. It was in the rubber plantation area that absolute mansions were beheld! Evidently rubber plantations produce a wealthy crop.

Once settled in a one star hotel in Monnar, Vanesh drove us to Eravikelam National Park where we had to take a bus to the park and then walk a kilometer or so to view some Nilgiri tahr (a type of mountain goat).

Next on his itinerary was a horticultural garden that was thoroughly engaging. He knew where to take us for the next stop was a dam that created a vast lake. Then on to Echo Point where as its name suggests, one can speak and the echo returns.

That evening he suggested we drive back twenty-nine kilometers to take in a Kerala show of dancing and of martial arts. The latter did not interest me, but it turned out to be extremely exciting. Such agility and liveliness! The conclusion was four of the athletes diving through three rings of fire. The dance proved disappointing compared to the one I remember in Kerala in 1989.

Vanesh even drove us to a restaurant and waited until we had eaten before taking us back to the hotel. As we were unhappy with the hotel, we did not stay the booked two nights but next day Vanesh drove to Thekkety instead. Although much more expensive we had a much more comfortable hotel! En route we viewed a couple of waterfalls besides the one in the town itself. We also stopped to see where someone had placed his coffee beans to dry on the side of the road. However tea plantations in the reddish soil were the prevalent crop.

We also stopped at a spice garden for a half hour tour. I tried to make notes, but our guide went too quickly. Sweet limes were so large and I had no idea that the cocoa pod is as large as it is. Black pepper seeds produce black, green and white pepper. We tasted several leaves. We were shown three types of coffee bushes: the only one, the best, Arabia is exported. It would seem that the Indians have a herb or spice for everything that ails one.

I had hoped to return to Madurai, but because of a dispute between Kerala and Tamil Nadu over some ninety-nine agreement pact over some dam, Vanesh felt it not safe to travel there. It required the driver to register his passengers when we crossed from one state to another. (And as aside Vanesh had to return through the same border crossings he had driven us; no cutting across country!)

I might mention we witnessed an eclipse of a full moon in this area. We viewed a myriad of aspects: pasture land on the hills, cattle with white herons nearby, olive palm trees, jack fruit trees, more rubber plantations with the accompanying mansions, vividly coloured houses, churches with people in their finery walking to church, CPI painted on rocks or red flags denoting the Communist party, STOP signs and often traffic lights for the most part that meant nothing, pot-holed roads to fine highways.

The travel agent manager alerted Vanesh that we did not have to make an intermediary stop: he had arranged we could go right through to Kodaikanal which meant a three hundred kilometer drive for Vanesh. As he was a smoker, he did stop occasionally. The road was good until the last sixty kilometers into Kodai, curves galore and pot-holed. Rice became the predominant crop replacing tea. Vanesh pointed out mango trees, cashew nut trees, a tire factory, mosques and a Hindu temple atop a hill Probably the most spectacular aspect was the number of wind turbines.

We, in southern Alberta have a number of them, but nothing like the hundreds that were spread over a number of kilometers in Tamil Nadu!

Kodai has changed greatly to a large town from the time Tom and I were there. We picked up a guide and visited several areas. However at one point at six thousand feet we were in the clouds and could only get a glimpse of the pillar rock. A hill station, it is noted for its moderate day-time temperature.

We drove another two hundred plus kilometers to Ooty, another hill station. Once we had driven down the horrific road from Kodai, the highway was quite smooth. We passed though a large centre, Tirupur, where we noted an eye foundation and knitting mills. The winding road to Ooty was not near as bad as the one to Kodai. However, small monkeys were most prolific. Like Kodai, Ooty had changed greatly: the biggest difference being that whereas we used to be able to walk leisurely around the lake, now it is fenced off and one has to rent a boat to be near the lake.

Our first stop next morning was at the rose garden which won the international prize in 2005. But in December, it was far from its full glory, even though there were several lovely blooms. The botanical garden gave us an opportunity to walk for a change. We viewed bonsai trees of every variety, to huge trees and a huge gnarled, fossilised root that rose up out of the ground. Very interesting!

We departed Ooty via another route that had thirty-six numbered curves! We drove through a tiger preserve, but no sign of a tiger. Although there was elephant dung on the road, we did not see an elephant either. We did see small termite hills and the monkeys were prevalent as well.

We had a one night stay at some cottages to break the trip to Mysore where we actually had the chance to be lazy! Soon we were to cross into the state of Karnaka. We saw windrows of hay being gathered up by both male and female. Also on the highway were the loads of hay either transported by truck or oxen-driven carts. We also saw sugar cane growing.

I guess the trips I have made to Mysore I had forgotten how beautiful its interior is. The only thing in my travels can I find comparable would be Versailles or Schobrunn. The British really outdid themselves re-building it after a fire. We had to check our shoes and cameras and yet there were several Indians taking pictures with their cellular phones. The golden howdah used for parades and weighing seven hundred fifteen kilograms was a sight to behold. To describe it is almost impossible: teak carved doors and ceilings, the paintings, tapestries with silver thread, elaborately painted ceilings, the long hall for entertainment, the children's swimming pool, chandeliers, and the symmetrical archways.

Again we had to pay ten times as much as natives to enter the museum to view old means of transportation, hunting trophies, swords and long-barrelled guns. I could have skipped it!

The afternoon was spent shopping, particularly in a silk shop next to our five star hotel where I was measured for a skirt and jacket. It was probably slightly more expensive there, but I also thought it more reliable. I was happy with it next day!

The next morning Vanesh drove us up a winding road to a famous Hindu temple. But after removing our shoes and queuing, we found as non-Hindus we could not enter and had to view it from several meters away. What we saw was Mysore's smog en route!

The day before on our way into Mysore I had noted a Hindu complex on the outskirts of the city. I asked Vanesh to drive there, only to find a padlock on the gate. But Vanesh was able to speak to the caretaker and we were allowed entrance. The first object of interest was a huge black idol of some Hindu god. Then we were led around the fifty shrines on the property. The old ones are six hundred years old while the newer ones are one hundred years old. Some of the smaller ones are constructed on the back of a turtle. Their feet and head are clearly visible. Unfortunately vandals had "chopped" off many heads of the turtles. No wonder they kept the gate locked with barbed wire around the perimeter.

Vanesh then drove us to Brindavan Gardens. It in no way resembled what I remembered from 1989! There are still lots of steps to navigate, but a lot of water ways and more fountains have been added. I suppose going in the evening might have been better, but it was a Sunday and I did want to witness the Mysore palace illuminated as I had seen it the once before in 1989. What adjectives to describe it: superb, dazzling, magnificent, simply beautiful!

Vanesh kept his promise to have dinner with us the final night. I think he hated to leave us as much as we hated to leave him! He had mentioned before a girlfriend he liked, but that night he told us his parents had chosen a distant relative for him to marry after his twenty-eighth birthday at the end of February. Just does not seem fair to me! But at least it is not an older man-child marriage as some still are.

We had a great wide highway to Bangalore where that evening we were to meet our friends, Adil and Kashmin, again. Bangalore is the Silicon Valley of India, truly a booming city. There are malls that revel anything in North America.

One tourist attraction that Kashmin drove us to was the palace that has only been open to the public two or three years. It is the summer palace of the "king" of Mysore. He had a penchant for nudes; hence many lovely paintings of nudes.

Soon it was time to pack our bags and travel to the new airport that is forty kilometres from the city. Again, progress.

EPILOGUE

I love the Indian people. I believe they like us as well. How many times have they asked to have their pictures taken with us with their cameras? I guess it is because our skin is white.

The Indians are a clever race. (I have had two Indian medical doctors in my small town.) Why is it that internet companies are outsourcing to India? Yes, because it is economical, but also because they are capable of handling the problems. There are many institutes of various types around the country of India.

However, as I have indicated, the traffic is ferocious! First of all lane changing means nothing. Traffic rules mean nothing. As Adil has stated Might is Right. The larger vehicles definitely take precedence over anything smaller.

Sadly the poverty is still there. Some still sleep on the sidewalks or live in shacks. But regrettably, we in Canada, have our poor as well. Whether it was the areas we were in this last trip, but I did not think we encountered as many beggars as other years.

But what we did contend with was GARBAGE! It is a shame for some beautiful areas to be impaired by so much trash. The Indians have a lot to learn in that aspect!

One sees very few old cars on the road. It seems as if everyone is driving modern vehicles. In other words India had made great progress in the past twenty years.

IF INDIA IS NOT QUITE BLOSSOMING, IT CERTAINLY IS IN AN INTRIGUING BUDDING STAGE.

The author, widowed in 1985, a retired school teacher, has travelled to India seven times. She loves to travel but is running out of safe countries to visit. She has a married daughter with two sons and is now a great grandmother of two boys. Her son is unmarried. She swims three times a week and likes to snorkel when visiting a tropical country.